Fantasy
MERMAIDS

COLORING BOOK

Fantasy Mermaids Coloring Book

ISBN: 9798618431460

www.colormoodbooks.com

BOOKS

Thank you for your purchase!

If you've had a pleasant buying experience, we want to let you know that
your feedback means the world to us.

We would be extremely grateful if you could leave us a positive feedback with
5 stars service rating

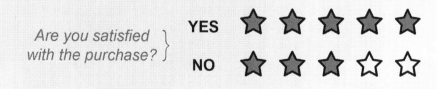

Regards,

COLORMOOD Books

Our other books

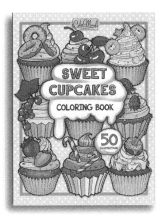

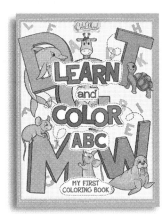

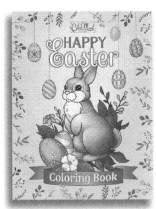

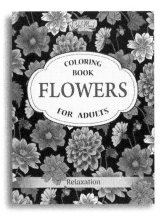

+ Follow

www.colormoodbooks.com